Key Stage 1 English Practice Tes

CU00820032

Author: Rachel Axten-Higg

Contents

Instructions 2

Answers 4

Set A

English Reading Paper 1: Reading Prompt and Answer Booklet 17

English Reading Paper 2: Reading Booklet 31

English Reading Paper 2: Reading Answer Booklet 39

English Grammar, Punctuation and Spelling Paper 1: Spelling 47

English Grammar, Punctuation and Spelling Paper 2: Questions 51

Set B

English Reading Paper 1: Reading Prompt and Answer Booklet 63

English Reading Paper 2: Reading Booklet 77

English Reading Paper 2: Reading Answer Booklet 85

English Grammar, Punctuation and Spelling Paper 1: Spelling 93

English Grammar, Punctuation and Spelling Paper 2: Questions 97

Instructions

Introduction

This practice resource consists of two complete sets of Key Stage 1 English practice test papers. Each set contains test papers similar to those that pupils will take at the end of Year 2:

- **Reading** – each test is made up of two papers. Paper 1 requires the child to read a number of short pieces of text and then answer two or three questions on each piece of text. Paper 2 consists of three different texts (in a reading booklet), and an answer booklet.

- **Grammar, Punctuation and Spelling** – each test is made up of Paper 1 and Paper 2. Paper 1 contains 20 spellings within the context of sentences. The spelling test administration guides can be found on pages 8 and 14 of this answer booklet. Paper 2 consists of grammar and punctuation questions.

These test papers can be used at any time throughout the year to provide practice for the Key Stage 1 tests.

Administering the Tests

- Children should work in a quiet environment where they can complete each test undisturbed and you can give the prompts required.

- You need to explain each test and go through the practice questions by reading them aloud, allowing children to answer the questions, and then working through the answers with them. In the reading test it is particularly important that you check children are reading the text in order to answer the questions and not thinking they have to answer from their own knowledge.

- The amount of time per test varies. The Key Stage 1 tests are not strictly timed and it is up to you to decide when or if a break is required during these practice tests. Below is a guide to approximately how long each test is expected to take:
  - **Reading Paper 1** – 30 minutes
  - **Reading Paper 2** – 40 minutes
  - **Grammar, Punctuation and Spelling Paper 1 (Spelling)** – 15 minutes
  - **Grammar, Punctuation and Spelling Paper 2 (Questions)**– 20 minutes

Marking the Tests

Each set of English practice papers contains two Reading papers and two Grammar, punctuation and spelling papers:

- Reading paper 1 is worth 20 marks.
- Reading paper 2 is worth 20 marks.

  Total = 40 marks

- Grammar, punctuation and spelling Paper 1 is worth 20 marks
- Grammar, punctuation and spelling Paper 2 is worth 20 marks

  Total = 40 marks

Use this answer booklet to mark the test papers.

Add up the total marks for the two Reading papers. As a general guideline, if a child gets 25 or more marks on the Reading papers, they are reaching the expected standard.

Add up the total marks for the two Grammar, punctuation and spelling papers. As a general guideline, if a child gets 24 or more marks across the two papers, they are reaching the expected standard.

Keep in mind that the exact number of marks required to achieve the expected standard may vary year by year depending on the overall difficulty of the test.

Answers

Content domain coverage for the questions in these papers are shown in the tables of answers below. Information about these codes can be found in the KS1 English test framework.

Set A
Reading – Paper 1

Question (Content domain)		Requirement	Mark
Practice Questions		*a. Freddie* *b. excited*	
1	(1d)	Award 1 mark for **He needed to take it to school to wear for Sports Day**.	1
2	(1b, 1d)	Award 1 mark for reference to his face being covered in spots, e.g. • he had spots • he had spots on his face • he had a spotty face. Do not accept reference to his reflection in the mirror without mention of spots on his face.	1
3	(1b)	Award 1 mark for reference to two of the following: • ran (upstairs) • looked at his face • told him he had chickenpox • put her arms around him/Freddie • hugged him/Freddie.	1
4	(1b)	Award 1 mark for **Eliza**.	1
5	(1a, 1d)	Award 1 mark for **He did not want to play with his cars or make models**.	1
6	(1b)	Award 1 mark for reference to being at school Sports Day, e.g. • winning his races • going to school for Sports Day • running in the races. Do not accept negative answers that do not positively identify that he wants to be at Sports Day, e.g. • not being at home • not making models.	1
7	(1b)	Award 1 mark for identifying that they watched the Guinea Pig Sports Day, e.g. • they watched the guinea pigs race • the guinea pigs had a Sports Day • to watch Freddie do races for the guinea pigs. Do not accept reference to the weather being warm.	1
8	(1d)	Award 1 mark for **happy**.	1
9	(1b)	Award 1 mark for: | Sentence	True	False
---	---	---
Freddie doesn't like Sports Day at school.		✓
Freddie has pet guinea pigs.	✓	
Freddie's mum made a model with him at home.		✓		1

Question (Content domain)		Requirement	Mark
Practice Questions		*a. Summer Olympics and Winter Olympics* *b. watched*	
10	(1b)	Award 1 mark for reference to a running race.	1 **5**
11	(1b)	Award 1 mark for **Greece**.	1
12	(1b)	Award 1 mark for two of the following: • boxing • long jump • javelin. Do not accept other events that have been added but are not mentioned in the text.	1
13	(1b)	Award 1 mark for reference to men, e.g. • only men • men. Also accept "not women".	1
14	(1b)	Award 1 mark for both of the following: • hope • peace.	1
15	(1b)	Award 1 mark for **1900**.	1
16	(1a, 1d)	Award 1 mark for **France**.	1
17	(1b)	Award 1 mark for one of the following: • Athens • Greece • Athens in Greece.	1
18	(1a)	Award 1 mark for **improve**.	1
19	(1b)	Award 1 mark for **represent your country**.	1
20	(1b)	Award 1 mark for: First — gold Second — silver Third — bronze	1

Set A
Reading – Paper 2

Question (Content domain)		Requirement	Mark
1	(1b)	Award 1 mark for **bees and wasps**.	1
2	(1b)	Award 1 mark for any two of the following: • head • thorax • abdomen • legs • feelers • hooked claws.	1
3	(1b)	Award 1 mark for any two of the following: • worker • soldier • drone • queen.	1
4	(1b)	Award 1 mark for reference to cocoon or chrysalis.	1
5a	(1b)	Award 1 mark for **drone(s)**.	1
5b	(1b)	Award 1 mark for **queen(s)**.	1
6	(1b)	Award 1 mark for: Leafcutter ants — teach other ants to find food Honeypot ants — give out liquid food to others Rock ants — bring leaves to feed to a special fungus (Leafcutter ants → bring leaves to feed to a special fungus; Honeypot ants → give out liquid food to others; Rock ants → teach other ants to find food)	1
7	(1b)	Award 1 mark for three boxes correctly ticked and award 2 marks for all four boxes correctly ticked. <table><tr><th>Sentence</th><th>True</th><th>False</th></tr><tr><td>Greenfly make a liquid called honeydew.</td><td>✓</td><td></td></tr><tr><td>Ants make a liquid called honeydew.</td><td></td><td>✓</td></tr><tr><td>Some ants keep caterpillars in their nests.</td><td>✓</td><td></td></tr><tr><td>Farmers keep ants in their barns overnight.</td><td></td><td>✓</td></tr></table>	Up to 2
8	(1b)	Award 1 mark for **on the floor**.	1
9	(1b)	Award 1 mark for reference to underground/below the ground, e.g. • in a nest underground • deep below the ground • under the ground.	1
10	(1b)	Award 1 mark for reference to any of the following: • grew wings and flew away • came from their nest • flew into the sky • flew away • grew wings and looked like flies.	1
11	(1d, 1b)	Award 1 mark for **live and change**.	1
12	(1b)	Award 1 mark for two of the following: • horses • ducks • goats. Do not accept more sheep.	1

Question (Content domain)		Requirement	Mark
13	(1a)	Award 1 mark for **sad and upset**.	1
14	(1d)	Award 1 mark for **The gate creaked**.	1
15	(1b)	Award 1 mark for reference to each of the following points, up to a maximum of 2 marks: • the sounds • (strange) shadows (on the floor). Also accept remembering/thinking of monster stories for 1 mark.	Up to 2
16	(1b)	Award 1 mark for **her voice**.	1
17	(1c)	Award 1 mark for: Gerty tells Samson she ran away from her farm [5] Samson is teased by the other animals. [1] Samson is scared in the woods. [3] Samson packs up his belongings. [2] Samson meets Gerty. [4]	1

Set A
Grammar, punctuation and spelling – Paper 1: spelling

Children should have a pen or pencil and a rubber to complete the paper.
They are not allowed to use a dictionary or electronic spell checker.

Ask children to look at the practice spelling question. Do this question together.

For each question, read out the word that they will need to spell correctly.
Then read the whole sentence.
Then read the word again.
Children need to write the word into the blank space in the sentence.

Here is the practice question for Set A:
*The word is **play**.*
*The children **play** in the park.*
*The word is **play**.*
Check that children understand that 'play' should be written in the blank space.

Explain that you are going to read 20 sentences. Each sentence has a word missing, just like the practice question.
Read questions 1 to 20, starting with the question number, then reading out the word followed by the sentence, and then the word again.

Leave enough time (at least 12 seconds) between questions for children to attempt the spelling. Do not rush, as the test time of 15 minutes is approximate and children will be given more time if they need it.

Children may cross out the word and write it again if they think they have made a mistake.
You may repeat the target word if needed.

Award **1 mark** for each correct spelling.

Practice: The word is **play**.
*The children **play** in the park.*
The word is **play**.

Spelling 1: The word is **farmyard**.
*The tractor is parked in the **farmyard**.*
The word is **farmyard**.

Spelling 2: The word is **hospital**.
*The doctor works in the **hospital**.*
The word is **hospital**.

Spelling 3: The word is **give**.
*I had to **give** her a sweet from my bag.*
The word is **give**.

Spelling 4: The word is **towards**.
*Head **towards** the park.*
The word is **towards**.

Spelling 5: The word is **reply**.
*I had to **reply** to the message.*
The word is **reply**.

Spelling 6: The word is **dinosaurs**.
***Dinosaurs** once lived on Earth.*
The word is **dinosaurs**.

Spelling 7: The word is **giraffe**.
*A **giraffe** has a long neck.*
The word is **giraffe**.

Spelling 8: The word is **miss**.
*It was hard to **miss** the target.*
The word is **miss**.

Spelling 9: The word is **television**.
*I watch the **television** in the evenings.*
The word is **television**.

Spelling 10: The word is **bottle**.
*There was a message in the **bottle**.*
The word is **bottle**.

Spelling 11: The word is **patting**.
*He was **patting** the dog gently.*
The word is **patting**.

Spelling 12: The word is **beautiful**.
*The princess was **beautiful**.*
The word is **beautiful**.

Spelling 13: The word is **brother**.
*I have a younger **brother**.*
The word is **brother**.

Spelling 14: The word is **fossil**.
*I found a **fossil** on the beach.*
The word is **fossil**.

Spelling 15: The word is **won**.
*He **won** the race on Sports Day.*
The word is **won**.

Spelling 16: The word is **chimney**.
*The smoke came out of the **chimney**.*
The word is **chimney**.

Spelling 17: The word is **bridge**.
*The goat crossed over the **bridge**.*
The word is **bridge**.

Spelling 18: The word is **party**.
*I had a **party** for my birthday.*
The word is **party**.

Spelling 19: The word is **babies**.
*The **babies** were all crying.*
The word is **babies**.

Spelling 20: The word is **gnawed**.
*The beaver **gnawed** the wood.*
The word is **gnawed**.

Set A

Grammar, punctuation and spelling – Paper 2: questions

Question *Content domain*		Requirement	Mark
Practice Questions		*a. helping* *b.* (my) *favourite colour is blue.*	
I	(G3)	Award I mark for **however**.	I
2	(G3)	Award I mark for the correct word circled. The children play in the water (if) it is warm.	I
3	(G5)	Award I mark for a comma after hats. The children had to bring hats, scarves and gloves.	I
4	(G5)	Award I mark for **full stop**.	I
5	(GI)	Award I mark for the correct word circled. The (gate) was creaking.	I
6	(G2)	Award I mark for **a question**.	I
7	(GI)	Award I mark for one plausible *–ly* adverb or one plausible adverb that does not end in *–ly*, e.g. • carefully • slowly • gently • badly • softly • today • often • yesterday. **Additional guidance:** • Spelling should not be assessed for the award of this mark.	I
8	(G5)	Award I mark for a response that explains that the words are capital letters because they are the personal pronoun I. Do not accept general responses, e.g. because they are important. **Additional guidance:** • Spelling should not be assessed for the award of this mark. • Sentence grammar and punctuation in the pupil's explanation should not be assessed for the award of this mark.	I
9	(G6)	Award I mark for all three correct. | Noun	Singular	Plural
---	---	---
bottle	✓	
shoes		✓
trees		✓		I
10	(GI)	Award I mark for **a verb**.	I
II	(G5)	Award I mark for **Isaac's painting has green keys on it**.	I
12	(G3)	Award I mark for **When**.	I
13	(GI)	Award I mark for the correct word circled. The children were (nearest) the snake.	I

Question *Content domain*		Requirement	Mark
14	(G5)	Award 1 mark for all three correct. The lions. like to sit in the sun. They have a big rock ◌ to sit on. The meat they are given ◌ to eat ◌ is hung up on ropes.	1
15a	(G4)	Award 1 mark for one plausible verb that forms the present progressive, e.g. • making • creating • inventing • showing. **Additional guidance:** • Responses must be spelt correctly.	1
15b	(G4)	Award 1 mark for one plausible simple past tense verb, e.g. • made • created • invented • showed. Do not accept done. **Additional guidance:** • Responses must be spelt correctly.	1
16	(G3, G5)	Award 2 marks for an appropriate, grammatically correct sentence, with correct use of capital letters and end punctuation, e.g. • The children are playing in the pool. • People are playing in the pool. • The children have a ball. • I can see people in the swimming pool. • There are six people in the pool. Award 1 mark for an appropriate, grammatically correct sentence, with incorrect use of capital letters and/or end punctuation, e.g. • people are in the pool • a girl is looking happy. • The people are enjoying the pool • The children like Playing in the pool. Do not accept a phrase (with or without correct punctuation) e.g. • a fun pool • children playing in the pool • a small swimming pool	Up to 2

17	(G6)	Award 1 mark for all three correct.
		
		thick ————————— ness
		                    ment
		bright ————————— ness
		                    ment
		                    ness
		move ————————— ment
			1

18	(G4)	Award 1 mark for all three correct. | Sentence	Past tense	Present tense
---	---	---
Ashif ate his lunch.	✓	
Ashif gives out knives and forks.		✓
Ashif thanked the cooks.	✓			1

Set B

Reading – Paper 1

Question (Content domain)		Requirement	Mark
Practice Questions		a. Wednesday b. A girl	
1	(1a)	Award 1 mark for **eating grass**.	1
2	(1b)	Award 1 mark for a reference to one of the following: • to keep them safe • so they didn't get eaten (by foxes).	1
3	(1a, 1b)	Award 1 mark for both words identified: • sticky • ugly. Do not accept references not from the text.	1
4	(1d)	Award 1 mark for **the fox**.	1
5	(1b)	Award 1 mark for reference to: • she had left Georgie • she had gone to look for worms.	1
6a	(1b)	Award 1 mark for reference to one of the following: • Mr Hendoodle was watching. • Mr Hendoodle was perched up high. • Mr Hendoodle was a good fighter.	1
6b	(1b)	Award 1 mark for 2/two.	1
7	(1a)	Award 1 mark for **sneaking**.	1
8	(1b)	Award 1 mark for **The fox dropped Georgie**.	1
9	(1c)	Award 1 mark for: The fox had Georgie in his mouth. [1] The fox dropped Georgie. [3] Mr Hendoodle hit the fox on the nose. [4] Mr Hendoodle dropped down. [2]	1
10	(1a)	Award 1 mark for **kiddo**.	1
11	(1b)	Award 1 mark for reference to one of the following: • perch • high perch	1
12	(1d)	Award 2 marks for reference to being saved from the fox <u>and</u> having a lovely family/having a dad who is a good fighter, e.g. • she was saved from the fox and her family look after her • she was saved from the fox and her dad is strong enough to fight off enemies. Award 1 mark for only one of the references above.	Up to 2
Practice Questions		a. eggs b. 3/three	
13	(1b)	Award 1 mark for **India**.	1
14	(1b)	Award 1 mark for reference to them laying an egg every day.	1
15	(1b)	Award 1 mark for **Spain**.	1
16	(1b)	Award 1 mark for **(over) 50 billion**. Award the mark even with spelling errors.	1
17	(1b)	Award 1 mark for **(more than) 34 million**. Award the mark even with spelling errors.	1
18	(1b)	Award 1 mark for two of following: • boiled • scrambled • fried • in other recipes/in cakes Do not accept answers not in the text.	1

Set B
Reading – Paper 2

Question (Content domain)		Requirement	Mark
1	(1b)	Award 1 mark for reference to any of the following acceptable points: • explains the difference between harmless dragons and ones that will eat you • gives you information about different types of dragons • tells you what to do to keep safe if you see one.	1
2	(1b)	Award 1 mark for **hide (quietly)**.	1
3	(1b)	Award 1 mark for any two of the following: • (do not) run • (do not) make any sudden movement • (do not) scream.	1
4	(1b)	Award 1 mark for both of the following: • (fight over) food • (fight over the) best nest site.	1
5	(1a)	Award 1 mark for **snout**.	1
6	(1b)	Award 1 mark for: Green dragons ——————— eat sheep or cows Black dragons ╲ ╱ the cleverest of all dragons Blue dragons ╱ ╲ some have two heads	1
7	(1b)	Award 1 mark for 3 boxes correctly ticked and award 2 marks for all 4 boxes correctly ticked. | Sentence	True	False
---	---	---
Only some dragons hatch from eggs.		✓
Wyrms come out of the water to form a cocoon.	✓	
It is hardest to kill a dragon when it is in the cocoon stage.		✓
Dragons newly hatched from cocoons do not have wings.		✓		Up to 2
8	(1b)	Award 1 mark for **a dragon**.	1
9	(1d)	Award 1 mark for reference to either of the following acceptable points: • he had a sword • he had a helmet.	1
10	(1b, 1d)	Award 2 marks for reference to there being no food left <u>and</u> the houses all being burned down, e.g. • the houses were burned by the dragon so there was no food in them • the dragon had destroyed everything, including the food and houses. Award 1 mark for reference to any of the following acceptable points: • the houses had been burned • there was no food left as the dragon had destroyed it • the dragon had destroyed everything.	Up to 2
11	(1b)	Award 1 mark for **He stepped backwards**.	1
12	(1b)	Award 1 mark for reference to flames and/or fire. Do not accept smoke.	1
13	(1d)	Award 1 mark for **Miggs**.	1
14a	(1d)	Award 1 mark for **strict**.	1
14b	(1d)	Award 1 mark for **thoughtful**.	1

Question (Content domain)		Requirement	Mark
15a	(1d)	Award 1 mark for reference to one of the following: • sad/upset • pleased/proud • relieved • confused.	1
15b	(1d, 1b)	Award 1 mark for any plausible text-based explanation for the feeling identified in part a, e.g. • (sad) because his model had gone • (pleased) because he had done what he had been told.	1
16	(1c)	Award 1 mark for all boxes numbered correctly: Niggle set fire to his model knight. [5] Mrs Forg shouted, "Stop that!". [1] Miggs set fire to his model knight. [4] Niggle tripped over his tail. [2] Niggle thought Mrs Forg might eat him. [3]	1

Set B
Grammar, punctuation and spelling – Paper 1: spelling

Children should have a pen or pencil and a rubber to complete the paper.
They are not allowed to use a dictionary or electronic spell checker.

Ask children to look at the practice spelling question. Do this question together.

For each question, read out the word that they will need to spell correctly.
Then read the whole sentence.
Then read the word again.
Children need to write the word into the blank space in the sentence.

Here is the practice question for Set B:
The word is **today**.
We are at school **today**.
The word is **today**.
Check that children understand that 'today' should be written in the blank space.

Explain that you are going to read 20 sentences. Each sentence has a word missing, just like the practice question.
Read questions 1 to 20, starting with the question number, then reading out the word followed by the sentence, and then the word again.

Leave enough time (at least 12 seconds) between questions for children to attempt the spelling. Do not rush, as the test time of 15 minutes is approximate and children will be given more time if they need it.

Children may cross out the word and write it again if they think they have made a mistake.
You may repeat the target word if needed.

Award **1 mark** for each correct spelling.

Practice: The word is **today**.
We are at school **today**.
The word is **today**.

Spelling 1: The word is **squirrel**.
The **squirrel** *climbed the tree.*
The word is **squirrel**.

Spelling 2: The word is **sunk**.
The boat was **sunk** *by pirates.*
The word is **sunk**.

Spelling 3: The word is **quickest**.
The boy won the race because he was the **quickest**.
The word is **quickest**.

Spelling 4: The word is **summer**.
We went on holiday in the **summer**.
The word is **summer**.

Spelling 5: The word is **sketch**.
I had to **sketch** *a picture of a flower.*
The word is **sketch**.

Spelling 6: The word is **shiny**.
The diamond was **shiny**.
The word is **shiny**.

Spelling 7: The word is **national**.
They sang the **national** *anthem for the Queen.*
The word is **national**.

Spelling 8: The word is **squash**.
I had a drink of orange **squash**.
The word is **squash**.

Spelling 9: The word is **rocks**.
The **rocks** *rolled down the hill.*
The word is **rocks**.

Spelling 10: The word is **village**.
A **village** *is smaller than a town.*
The word is **village**.

Spelling 11: The word is **elephant**.
The **elephant** *made a loud sound.*
The word is **elephant**.

Spelling 12: The word is **kitchen**.
I cooked a meal in the **kitchen**.
The word is **kitchen**.

Spelling 13: The word is **happiest**.
I am **happiest** *when eating chocolate.*
The word is **happiest**.

Spelling 14: The word is **always**.
I **always** *work hard at school.*
The word is **always**.

Spelling 15: The word is **happily**.
They walked **happily** *to school.*
The word is **happily**.

Spelling 16: The word is **worm**.
The **worm** *burrowed in the mud.*
The word is **worm**.

Spelling 17: The word is **jumping**.
He was **jumping** *for joy.*
The word is **jumping**.

Spelling 18: The word is **Thursday**.
Thursday *is a day of the week.*
The word is **Thursday**.

Spelling 19: The word is **city**.
London is the capital **city** *of England.*
The word is **city**.

Spelling 20: The word is **wrap**.
I had to **wrap** *the present.*
The word is **wrap**.

Set B

Grammar, punctuation and spelling – Paper 2: questions

Question *Content domain*		Requirement	Mark
Practice *Questions*		*a. played/climbed/went/got/were, etc.* *b. The(steps)were slippery.*	15
I	*(G3)*	Award I mark for **the small dog**.	I
2	*(G3)*	Award I mark for **if**.	I
3	*(G2)*	Award I mark for **a statement**.	I
4	*(G6)*	Award I mark for the correctly identified prefix **un-**	I
5	*(G6)*	Award I mark for the correctly identified suffix **–est**	I
6	*(GI)*	Award I mark for two correctly circled adverbs. I(gently)rocked the baby as she screamed(loudly.)	I
7	*(G2, G5)*	Award 2 marks for a grammatically correct question that uses correct question syntax, with correct use of initial capital letter and question mark, e.g. • When did dinosaurs live? • What did dinosaurs eat? • What was the name of the biggest one? • What colour were they? Award I mark for an appropriate question using correct question syntax, with incorrect use of initial capital letter and/or demarcation, e.g. • How did dinosaurs die out • were they scary. • how many babies did they have? • Were dinosaurs Happy? Do not accept a question not in context (with or without correct punctuation), e.g. • What did you have for tea last night? • When is lunchtime. **Additional guidance:** • Spelling should not be assessed for the award of this mark. • Incorrect use of punctuation other than capital letters and question mark should not be penalised.	Up to 2
8	*(GI)*	Award I mark for **a noun**.	I
9	*(G2)*	Award I mark for **Be quiet now**.	I
10	*(G2)*	Award I mark for all three correct. How many legs does a duck have [?] What a fantastic painting [!] Why are you crying [?]	I
II	*(GI)*	Award I mark for the correctly circled word. Ahmed(ran) to his wooden peg.	I
12	*(G4)*	Award I mark for **The child is playing on the swing**.	I
13	*(GI)*	Award I mark for both nouns correctly identified. I walked happily to school in the beautiful sunshine.	I

Question *Content domain*		Requirement	Mark
14	(G5)	Award 1 mark for a response that explains that the words start with a capital letter because they are at the start of the sentences. Do not accept general responses, e.g. because they are important. **Additional guidance:** • Spelling should not be assessed for the award of this mark. • Sentence grammar and punctuation in the pupil's explanation should not be assessed for the award of this mark.	1
15	(G5)	Award 1 mark for a comma after *Rachel.* Rachel, Freddie and Harley won the relay race.	1
16	(G5)	Award 1 mark for **an apostrophe**.	1
17	(G5)	Award 1 mark for the correctly written word *couldn't.* I **couldn't** eat all of my lunch.	1
18	(G5)	Award 1 mark for an apostrophe in Tim's. That is Tim's bike.	1
19	(G4)	Award 1 mark for **Sam rides on his bike**.	1

Key Stage 1

Set A

English reading

Paper 1: reading prompt and answer booklet

First Name	
Last Name	

Contents

The Guinea Pig Sports Day   Pages 19–24

The Olympic Games   Pages 25–30

Useful words

comb

guinea pig

The Guinea Pig Sports Day

When Freddie woke up on Wednesday morning he was super excited. The day that he had been waiting for had finally arrived. Sports Day! He was not all that good at writing, reading and maths (like his sister Lucy was) but he could run really fast. Sports Day was his day to shine!

Practice questions

a What is the name of the boy who could run very fast?

_____

b How did he feel about Sports Day?

Tick **one**.

worried ☐   surprised ☐

excited ☐   anxious ☐

Freddie pulled on his crumpled school uniform. He put his neatly folded sports kit into his rucksack. All that was left was for him to comb his hair. He grabbed the comb, pulled it through his hair and checked his reflection in the mirror.

"Aggghhh!" he cried.

His face was covered in spots.

---

1 Why did Freddie pack his sports kit into his rucksack?

Tick **one**.

He was going to play football with his friends. ☐

He wanted to hide the sports kit from his mum. ☐

He needed to take it to school to wear for Sports Day. ☐

He was going to the park to play on the equipment. ☐

○ 1 mark

2 Why did Freddie cry "Aggghhh!"?

_____

○ 1 mark

Freddie's mum, Eliza, came running up the stairs when she heard him scream. She looked at his face.

"Oh dear, you've got chickenpox," she said.

"It's not fair," whimpered Freddie. "The one day I really want to go to school and I can't."

Eliza put her arms around Freddie and hugged him.

---

3 Write **two** things Freddie's mum did when she heard him scream.

1. _____

2. _____

1 mark

4 What is Freddie's mum called?

Tick **one**.

Freddie ☐   Eliza ☐

Clara ☐   Lucy ☐

1 mark

After breakfast, Freddie stared out of the window crossly. His mum suggested they make a model or play with his cars. Freddie shook his head.

"But you always like making models," she said.

"Not today," replied Freddie. "Today I want to be running and winning all my races!"

"I have an idea," said Freddie's mum. "Follow me into the garden."

---

5 *Freddie shook his head.*

What does this tell you about Freddie's response to his mum's suggestion that he play with his cars or make models?

Tick **one**.

He did not want to play with his cars or make models. ☐

He wanted to play with his cars or make models. ☐

He was cross with his mum for suggesting it. ☐

He never likes playing with cars or making models. ☐

1 mark

6 What does Freddie want to be doing today?

_____

1 mark

Later that afternoon, Freddie's mum and dad sat on chairs to watch the first ever Guinea Pig Sports Day. There was a running event, an obstacle race, a jumping race and more. The event ended with a prize-giving ceremony and it was all organised by a beaming Freddie.

"What a brilliant idea, Mum," Freddie said. "I even think it beats winning a race on Sports Day! My guinea pigs love to be sporty, just like me!"

---

7 Why did Freddie's mum and dad sit in the garden in the afternoon?

_____

_____

○ 1 mark

8 How was Freddie feeling at the prize-giving?

Tick **one**.

nervous ☐   happy ☐

unhappy ☐   unsure ☐

○ 1 mark

9 Think about the **whole story**.

Put ticks in the table to show which of these sentences are **true** and which are **false**.

Sentence	True	False
Freddie doesn't like Sports Day at school.		
Freddie has pet guinea pigs.		
Freddie's mum made a model with him at home.		

○ 1 mark

Useful words

Olympics

Greece

javelin

Emperor

modern

Athens

The Olympic Games

Have you ever watched the Olympic Games? There are lots of events that take place in the modern Olympics. There are Summer Olympics and Winter Olympics. Each Olympics takes place every four years.

Practice questions

a **Find** and **copy** the **two** types of Olympic Games.

1. _____

2. _____

b Which word means the same as *viewed*?

Tick **one**.

events ☐   modern ☐

watched ☐   place ☐

The very first Olympic Games was held in 776BC. It took place in Olympia in the country of Greece. It only had one race, which was a running race. Over the years more events were added including boxing, long jump and javelin.

10 What was the one race in the first Olympics?

_____

○ 1 mark

11 In which country did the first Olympics take place?

Tick **one**.

Olympia ☐   Greece ☐

Athens ☐   England ☐

○ 1 mark

12 **Find** and **copy two** events that were added to the Olympics.

1. _____

2. _____

○ 1 mark

In the past, only men were allowed to take part in the Olympics. The prize was a crown of olive leaves. This was a sign of hope and peace. The Olympics stopped in 393AD when the Roman Emperor said they had to.

13 In the past, who was allowed to take part in the races?

_____

○
1 mark

14 **Find** and **copy two** things that the crown was a sign of.

1. _____

2. _____

1 mark

In 1894 a French man decided to start the Olympics again. The first modern Olympic Games was held in 1896. It took place in Athens in Greece. No women were allowed to take part until the next Games in 1900.

---

15 In which year were women allowed to take part in the modern Olympics?

Tick **one**.

1894 ☐   1900 ☐

1896 ☐   1996 ☐

1 mark

16 Which country did the man who restarted the Olympics come from?

Tick **one**.

Greece ☐   England ☐

Athens ☐   France ☐

1 mark

17 Where did the Olympics take place in 1896?

_____

1 mark

Athletes train hard between Olympics so they can try to improve and win their event. It is a big honour to represent your country at the Olympics. Medals are awarded to the people who come first (gold), second (silver) and third (bronze) in each event.

18 **Find** and **copy one** word that means the same as *get better*.

_____

1 mark

19 What is it an honour to do at the Olympics?

Tick **one**.

win every event ☐   get a medal for fourth place ☐

represent your country ☐   train hard between Olympics ☐

1 mark

20 Draw **three** lines to match these positions with the colour of the medal given.

First	bronze
Second	gold
Third	silver

1 mark

End of test

Ants

Ant Poem

There in a Wood...

Reading Booklet

Key Stage 1
Set A, Paper 2, English Reading Booklet

Contents

Ants   Pages 33–35

Ant Poem   Page 36

There in a Wood...   Pages 37–38

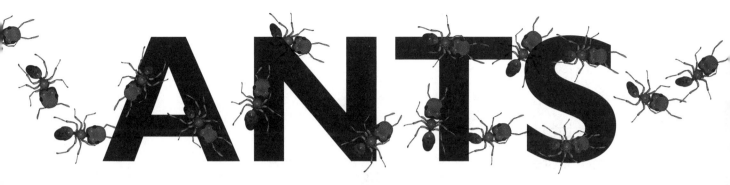

ANTS

Ants are insects that are related to bees and wasps.

Ants' bodies are made up of 3 parts – the head, the thorax and the abdomen. They have 6 legs, each ending in a hooked claw, which helps them to climb. They have 2 feelers on the tops of their heads.

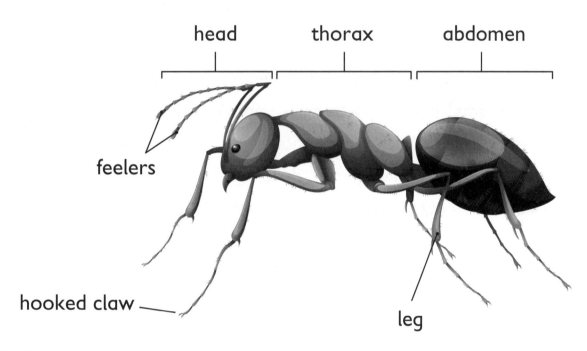

head   thorax   abdomen

feelers

hooked claw

leg

Colonies

Like most bees and wasps, ants live in large groups called colonies.

Ant colonies are different sizes in different parts of the world, with some colonies being very small (with just a few insects) whilst others have millions of insects.

Ant colonies are usually set up so that each ant has a job: worker, soldier, drone or queen.

Life cycles

All ants hatch from eggs. At first, they are a larva (a bit like a very small caterpillar). After some time, they will form a pupa (a bit like a cocoon or chrysalis). It is from this pupa that the "ant" that we all know will come.

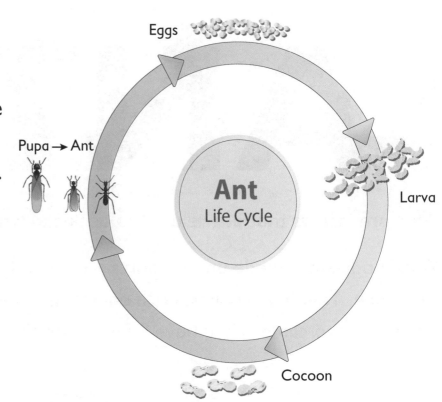

Eggs

Pupa → Ant

Larva

Ant
Life Cycle

Cocoon

At a particular time in the year, new queen and drone ants (sometimes called "flying ants" because they have wings) come out from their nests. These ants fly into the sky, where they mate, before landing again. The drones will die but the new queens drop their wings and begin to dig new nests and lay eggs. This is how ants spread to form new colonies.

Ants from around the world

Ants are found all over the world except for Antarctica and a few remote islands.

Here is some information about some of the different ants out there.

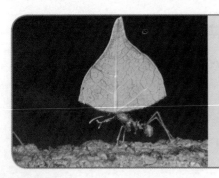

Leafcutter Ants

Leafcutter ants cut leaves and bring them back inside their nest, where they are fed to a special fungus that grows inside the nest. The fungus produces food, which the leafcutter ants eat and feed to their larvae.

Honeypot Ants

Large worker honeypot ants are over-fed by other workers until they get so fat that they cannot move. Once this happens the "fat ants" act as food stores for the other ants. When a worker needs some food, it strokes a "fat ant" which then gives out some of the liquid food stored in its stomach!

Rock Ants

Rock ants have been seen teaching each other where to find food. The rock ant that has discovered food will find another ant and then teach them the way back to the food by running with them and showing them the way!

Do ants keep pets?

Well, not exactly, but ants do look after some other insects that provide them with food. Find out more below.

Greenfly

Greenfly make a sweet sticky liquid called honeydew, which ants collect. Ants will look after greenfly, keeping ladybirds (that would try to eat the greenfly) away from them – a bit like a farmer keeping a wolf away from his sheep!

Caterpillars

Some other ants keep caterpillars inside their nests because they also produce honeydew. They take the caterpillars out during the day to nearby leaves where they can feed, before bringing them back into their nests overnight! This is a bit like a farmer taking his cows into the fields during the day and bringing them back to the barn at night.

Ant Poem

I was always interested in watching ants,
As they marched about the floor,
Like little soldiers, carrying their gear
Or going out to war.

I liked to watch their lines,
Heading back into the nest,
I'd watch them coming in and out,
And wonder if they'd ever rest.

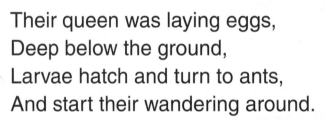

Their queen was laying eggs,
Deep below the ground,
Larvae hatch and turn to ants,
And start their wandering around.

I watched the ants all summer long,
Each day they did their things,
Until one day a hundred ants
Each cloaked with silver wings

Came from within their nest so deep
And taking to the skies
Looked less like ants I'd ever seen
And far much more like flies.

There in a Wood...

Once, on a farm in the country, there lived a sheep, whose name was Samson. Samson was not a fat sheep, nor a big sheep, nor indeed the sort of sheep that any farmer would want to take to market to sell. Some might even say he was a runt.

The other sheep, horses, ducks and goats (who also lived on the farm) all teased Samson about his small size and this upset him. He hated living on the farm and one day he decided that he would run away.

After tying up all the things he owned in a small, spotted, red handkerchief, which he tied to the end of a stick, Samson marched down to the front gate of the farm. The bigger, fatter sheep watched him go, laughing and pointing at him. Samson simply looked the other way and tried hard not to cry.

When he reached the front gate, he took the thin piece of twine that held the gate shut and unhooked it from the gatepost. The gate swung open with a creak. Samson looked around him, suddenly scared that the farmer would see him and make him come back to his field. There was no sign from the farmhouse that the farmer was coming, so Samson put his pack over his shoulder and walked off, leaving the gate open.

After some time, Samson found himself alone in a wood. He had never been in a wood before and the sounds all around made him a little scared. The trees and branches made strange shadows on the floor that made him think of the monster stories the other animals used to tell him. He walked on until he came to a small cottage.

It was getting dark and Samson was sure that he did not want to spend the night alone in the wood, so he went to the door of the cottage and knocked. After a while, the door opened and to Samson's surprise another little sheep stood in the doorway.

"Who are you?" asked the little sheep, in a voice that told Samson she was a girl sheep.

"My name is Samson," replied Samson. "I am lost. Can I please come in?"

"Yes, yes. Please do. My name is Gerty," said the girl sheep.

Gerty took Samson by the hoof and brought him into the cottage.

It turned out that Gerty had run away from a farm herself when she was younger and had found this cottage quite empty and decided to live here all by herself. She had made a lovely cottage garden for herself. She liked Samson and asked if he would like to stay with her.

So the two little sheep settled down to live happily ever after in the little cottage in the wood. And after a few years, neither of them was so little anymore.

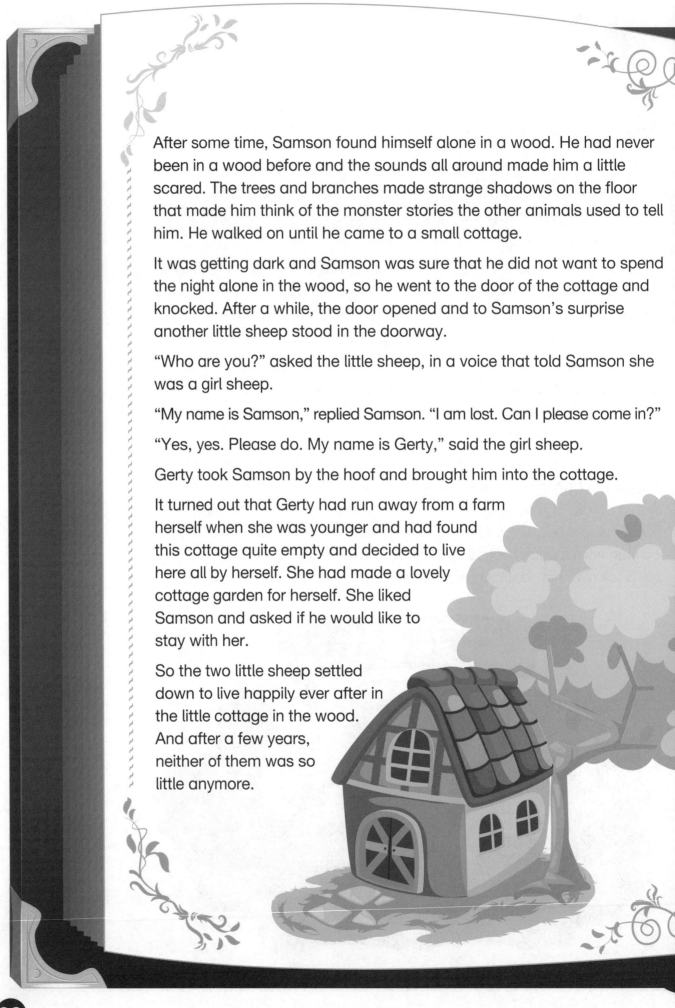

Key Stage 1

Set A

English reading

Paper 2: reading answer booklet

First Name	
Last Name	

(page 33)

1 Ants are related to...

Tick **one**.

bees and wasps ☐

beetles and earwigs ☐

bees and beetles ☐

wasps and ladybirds ☐

○ 1 mark

(page 33)

2 **Find** and **write two** parts of an ant's body.

1. _____

2. _____

○ 1 mark

(page 33)

3 Look at the **Colonies** section.

Write down **two** of the jobs that an ant in a colony might have.

1. _____

2. _____

○ 1 mark

(page 34)

4 What is a *pupa* similar to?

_____ 1 mark

(page 34)

5 Some ants in the colony fly into the sky.

What type of ant:

(a) ...dies when it lands again?

_____ 1 mark

(b) ...digs a nest and lays eggs?

_____ 1 mark

(pages 34–35)

6 Draw **three** lines to match these ants to what the text says about them.

Leafcutter ants	teach other ants to find food
Honeypot ants	give out liquid food to others
Rock ants	bring leaves to feed to a special fungus

1 mark

7 Put ticks in the table to show which sentences are **true** and which are **false**.

Sentence	True	False
Greenfly make a liquid called honeydew.		
Ants make a liquid called honeydew.		
Some ants keep caterpillars in their nests.		
Farmers keep ants in their barns overnight.		

2 marks

(page 36)

8 The poet saw the ants…

Tick **one**.

on the floor ☐

deep underground ☐

in the kitchen ☐

up a tree ☐

1 mark

(page 36)

9 Where did the queen lay the eggs?

_____

1 mark

(page 36)

10 What happened to the ants at the end of the summer?

_____

_____

1 mark

11 The poem explains how ants…

Tick **one**.

live and change ☐

fight like soldiers ☐

lay eggs ☐

play with humans ☐

1 mark

(page 37)

12 What animals other than sheep lived on the farm?

Write **two** answers.

1. _____

2. _____   1 mark

(page 37)

13 *Samson simply looked the other way and tried hard not to cry.*

What does this sentence tell you about how Samson is feeling?

Tick **one**.

proud and upset ☐   sad and upset ☐

proud and happy ☐   sad and excited ☐   1 mark

(page 37)

14 What happened to make Samson worried that the farmer might see him?

Tick **one**.

He shouted goodbye. ☐   The other sheep laughed. ☐

The gate creaked. ☐   The farmer was looking. ☐   1 mark

(page 38)

15 Samson did not like some of the things in the wood. As well as it being dark, what other things scared him?

Write **two**.

1. _____

2. _____

(page 38)

2 marks

16 What was it about the sheep at the door that made Samson think it was a girl?

Tick **one**.

her clothes ☐   her voice ☐

her hat ☐   the bow in her hair ☐

1 mark

(pages 37–38)

17 Number the following from 1 to 5 to show the order things happen in the story.

The first one has been done for you.

Gerty tells Samson she ran away from her farm. ☐

Samson is teased by the other animals. ☐ 1

Samson is scared in the woods. ☐

Samson packs up his belongings. ☐

Samson meets Gerty. ☐

1 mark

End of test

46

Key Stage 1

Set A

English grammar, punctuation and spelling

Paper 1: spelling

First Name	
Last Name	

Spelling

P.   The children _____ in the park.

1.   The tractor is parked in the _____.

2.   The doctor works in the _____.

3.   I had to _____ her a sweet from my bag.

4.   Head _____ the park.

5.   I had to _____ to the message.

6.   _____ once lived on Earth.

7.   A _____ has a long neck.

8.   It was hard to _____ the target.

9.   I watch the _____ in the evenings.

10. There was a message in the _____.

11. He was _____ the dog gently. ⭕

12. The princess was _____. ⭕

13. I have a younger _____. ⭕

14. I found a _____ on the beach. ⭕

15. He _____ the race on Sports Day. ⭕

16. The smoke came out of the _____. ⭕

17. The goat crossed over the _____. ⭕

18. I had a _____ for my birthday. ⭕

19. The _____ were all crying. ⭕

20. The beaver _____ the wood. ⭕

End of spelling test

BLANK PAGE

Key Stage I

Set A

English grammar, punctuation and spelling

Paper 2: questions

First Name	
Last Name	

Practice questions

a Tick the correct word to complete the sentence below.

We were _____ to bake some cakes.

Tick **one**.

helped ☐

help ☐

helps ☐

helping ☐

b Circle the word in the sentence below that must have a capital letter.

my favourite colour is blue.

1 Tick the correct word to complete the sentence below.

It is nice to play in the sun, _____ you should not play in it for too long.

Tick **one**.

if ☐

and ☐

or ☐

however ☐

1 mark

2 Circle **one** word in the sentence below that can be replaced with the word <u>when</u>.

The children play in the water if it is warm.

1 mark

3 Add one **comma** to the sentence below in the correct place.

The children had to bring hats scarves and gloves.

1 mark

4 Which punctuation mark completes the sentence below?

My favourite pet is a rabbit

Tick **one**.

full stop ☐

exclamation mark ☐

question mark ☐

comma ☐

1 mark

5 Circle the **noun** in the sentence below.

The gate was creaking.

○ 1 mark

6 What is the sentence below? The end punctuation is covered.

Is this your jumper

Tick **one**.

a statement ☐

a command ☐

an exclamation ☐

a question ☐

○ 1 mark

7 Write one **adverb** to complete the sentence below.

We threw the ball _____.

1 mark

8 Why are the underlined words **capital letters**?

On Wednesday I had to eat my breakfast quickly as I had to be at school early for my piano lesson.

_____

_____

1 mark

9 Tick to show whether each noun is **singular** or **plural**.

Noun	Singular	Plural
bottle		
shoes		
trees		

10 What type of word is underlined in the sentence below?

We heard the birds <u>singing</u> in the trees.

Tick **one**.

a verb ☐

a noun ☐

an adjective ☐

an adverb ☐

11 Which sentence uses an **apostrophe** correctly?

© HarperCollinsPublishers Ltd, 2018

Tick **one**.

Isaac's painting has green keys on it. ☐

Isaacs' painting has green keys on it. ☐

Isaacs painting has green key's on it. ☐

Isaacs painting has green keys' on it. ☐

○
1 mark

12 Tick the correct word to complete the sentence below.

_____ you are quiet, we can watch the film.

Tick **one**.

And ☐

However ☐

When ☐

But ☐

○
1 mark

13 Circle the **adjective** in the sentence below.

The children were nearest the snake.

1 mark

14 Circle the **full stops** that are in the wrong places.
One has been done for you.

The lions⊙ like to sit in the sun. They have a big rock. to sit on. The meat they are given. to eat. is hung up on ropes.

1 mark

15 Write **one** verb to complete what each child is saying.

(a) Today, I am _____ a model.

(b) Last week, I _____ a model.

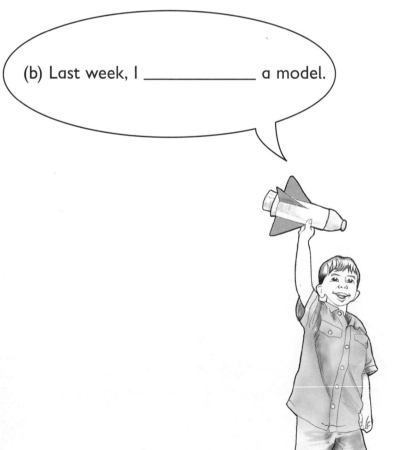

16 Write **one** sentence to describe something you see in the picture.

Remember to use the correct punctuation.

_____

_____

2 marks

17 Draw a line to match each word to the **suffix** that turns it into a noun.

Word   **Suffix**

                            ness

thick •   • ness
                            ment

                            ness

bright •   • ment

                            ness

move •   • ment

1 mark

18 Tick to show whether each sentence is written in the **past tense** or the **present tense**.

Sentence	Past tense	Present tense
Ashif ate his lunch.		
Ashif gives out knives and forks.		
Ashif thanked the cooks.		

1 mark

End of test

Key Stage 1

Set B

English reading

Paper 1: reading prompt and answer booklet

First Name	
Last Name	

Contents

Georgie Hendoodle   Pages 65–71

Chickens   Pages 72–76

Useful words

meadow

graze

beady

perched

luckiest

Georgie Hendoodle

As the little egg began to hatch, one fine Wednesday morning, the other little chicks stopped what they were doing to stare. Each of them had hatched from their eggs yesterday. Their little sister was late!

Practice questions

a When does the story start?

Tick **one**.

Monday ☐   Friday ☐

Wednesday ☐   Sunday ☐

b Was the chicken that was hatching a boy or a girl?

_____

Mr and Mrs Hendoodle lived on a farm. It was a small farm, not much more than three small fields and a little meadow, where Farmer Horris put the animals out to graze. The chickens lived in a coop next to the house. They were free to go in and out during the day, but the coop was closed up at night to keep them safe. As the late egg was hatching, a fox was watching. His beady eyes were fixed on the family gathered around the egg. He wanted to eat them all.

---

1 *...Farmer Horris put the animals out to graze.*

This means the animals were...

Tick **one**.

eating chicks ☐   playing ☐

eating grass ☐   shut in ☐

○ 1 mark

2 Why were the chickens shut up at night?

_____

○ 1 mark

After a little while, the eggshell dropped off and there lay the new-born chick, sticky and ugly – as all chicks are when they first hatch. Her mother came over and began cleaning her off. "We shall call her Georgie!" said Mrs Hendoodle. The new chick's brothers and sisters went back to playing.

The fox slunk closer.

Minutes after she had hatched, Georgie stood up, clean and ready to play. "Stay inside today," Mrs Hendoodle warned Georgie, "and don't wander off!"

---

3 **Find** and **copy two** words that describe the new-born chick.

1. _____

2. _____

○ 1 mark

4 What is a danger to Georgie?

Tick **one**.

the farmer ☐   the fox ☐

her brothers ☐   her sisters ☐

○ 1 mark

Mrs Hendoodle left Georgie and went off to look for worms to eat. Georgie looked around, thinking.

And that was when the fox pounced!

Unfortunately for the fox, Mr Hendoodle was watching. He had been perched up high looking down proudly at his new family below, when he saw the fox creeping up on the newly hatched Georgie. In his younger days, Mr Hendoodle had been a fantastic fighter. He had won his place in the farm by fighting off two other roosters who had tried to take the top spot.

---

5 Why was Mrs Hendoodle not there when the fox pounced?

_____

◯ 1 mark

6 (a) What was unfortunate for the fox?

_____

◯ 1 mark

(b) How many roosters had Mr Hendoodle fought off?

_____

◯ 1 mark

7 …*he saw the fox creeping up*…

The word *creeping* means…

Tick **one**.

sneaking ☐   dancing ☐

jumping ☐   running ☐

◯ 1 mark

The fox was planning to eat Georgie. He was not planning to be attacked by a rooster! Mr Hendoodle dropped from his perch and landed right in front of the fox. The fox jumped, dropping Georgie as he did so. As he landed back on the ground, Mr Hendoodle jumped up and kicked. The fox was hit on the nose by Mr Hendoodle's claws. This was too much for the fox, who turned and ran.

8 What happened when the fox jumped?

Tick **one**.

Mrs Hendoodle came back. ☐   Georgie got squashed. ☐

The fox dropped Georgie. ☐   Mr Hendoodle was squashed. ☐

9 Number the following events from 1 to 4 to show the order that they happened in the fight.

The first one has been done for you.

The fox had Georgie in his mouth. | 1 |

The fox dropped Georgie.   ☐

Mr Hendoodle hit the fox on the nose.   ☐

Mr Hendoodle dropped down.   ☐

Mr Hendoodle looked down at Georgie and frowned. "You gotta be careful out here kiddo! The farm can be a dangerous place!" he said, flapping his wings and jumping back up to his high perch.

Georgie looked around her and then trotted off to play with her brothers and sisters.

And so began the life of Georgie Hendoodle, luckiest chicken alive...

---

10 **Find** and **copy** the word that means *child.*

_____

1 mark

11 Where does Mr Hendoodle go back to?

_____

1 mark

12 Why is Georgie the luckiest chicken alive? Give **two** reasons.

_____

_____

2 marks

Useful words

billion

ancient

scrambled

Chickens

Chickens are birds that are kept by humans for meat and eggs. There are more chickens in the world than any other type of bird and there are over 19 billion of them worldwide, meaning there are nearly 3 chickens for every human on our planet.

Practice questions

a As well as meat, what are chickens kept for?

Tick **one**.

eggs ☐   friends ☐

feathers ☐   meat ☐

b How many chickens per human are there on our planet?

_____

Chickens in history

The first chickens to be kept by humans lived in India. They spread through trade to Ancient Egypt and Ancient Greece. In Ancient Egypt they were called "the bird that gives birth every day" because chickens lay an egg every day, which is different from other birds.

Chickens were brought to America, and to other parts of the world, by explorers from Spain. However, some people think that South Americans had already kept chickens before the Spanish arrived. It is difficult to say for certain.

---

13 In which country did humans first keep chickens?

_____

1 mark

14 What is different about chickens from other birds?

_____

15 Which country did the explorers come from who brought chickens to other parts of the world?

Tick **one**.

North America ☐   Spain ☐

South America ☐   Egypt ☐

Chickens in Farming

Humans eat chickens and this means that farms raise them in order to sell their meat to shops. In the United States over 50 billion chickens are raised for meat each year.

In the United Kingdom more than 34 million eggs are eaten per day. Eggs can be cooked and eaten in many different ways (for example boiled, scrambled or fried) and are also used in recipes such as cakes.

---

16 How many chickens are raised for meat in the United States per year?

_____

1 mark

17 How many eggs are eaten in the UK every day?

_____

1 mark

18 **Find** and **copy two** ways that eggs are eaten.

1. _____

2. _____

1 mark

End of test

A Dragon Spotter's Guide

The Day the Dragon Came

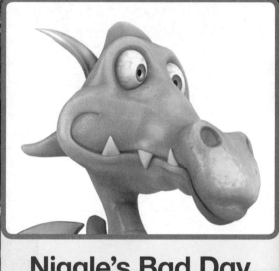

Niggle's Bad Day

Reading Booklet

Key Stage 1
Set B, Paper 2, English Reading Booklet

Contents

A Dragon Spotter's Guide   **Pages 79–81**

The Day the Dragon Came   **Page 82**

Niggle's Bad Day   **Pages 83–84**

A Dragon Spotter's Guide

Dragons can be a real problem if they come to live in your neighbourhood. This spotter's guide is designed to help you tell the difference between the harmless ones and the ones that will eat your whole family for breakfast!

Words of Wisdom

It is never wise to get too close to a dragon. Many have tried. A few have lived to tell the tale – but not many. If you do see a dragon, then the first thing to do is hide. Quietly. If you can get a good look at it, then do so – but only if it is safe. Do not make any sudden movement and whatever you do, do not run away! Dragons love to chase food and if they see you running away screaming, they will chase you and eat you on the spot.

Some Notes about Dragons

Dragons are large monsters. They live forever unless something or someone kills them. This happens very rarely. Usually a dragon is killed by another, bigger dragon because of some fight over food or the best nest site.

All dragons have scaly skin, which can be almost any colour from red to blue or even black. They have long tails and long necks. Their heads are similar to a crocodile's – they have a long snout filled with razor-sharp teeth. Their eyes face forward as do their nostrils. Many do not have ears, but instead have two holes on either side of their head. Dragons also have a pair of wings, which remain folded up at their sides when they are on the ground, but which will stretch out wide when flying. All dragons have four thick legs.

Different Types of Dragon

There are many different types of dragon. Below are some of the common dragons that you might see on your travels.

Green Dragons

Green dragons are a common sight in many countries around the world. Of all dragons, they have the shortest necks. They live in small groups of four or five beasts, often living in deserted valleys. They will raid farms for sheep or cows, carrying them off to eat in their nests. Green dragons will never attack humans – unless you go near their nests.

Blue Dragons

The cleverest of all dragons are the blue dragons. These creatures can talk but do not let this fool you. They do not understand what they are saying. They are a bit like parrots and just repeat what they hear. However, the trick is clever because humans will often think the dragons understand and that they can talk their way out of trouble, but the blue dragon is just using this as a way to keep the human still. After a short time, the dragon will attack.

Black Dragons

Black dragons are the strongest of all the different types of dragon. There have been several black dragons that have two heads, each at the end of a long, snake-like neck. They often have thick spikes all over their backs and their tails end in thick spikes too.

Life Cycle

Wyrm

All dragons hatch from eggs. At this point they are called wyrms (worms). These wyrms do not have wings, but have four strong legs, which they use to move themselves to water. They will spend the first four years of their lives living in a river or a lake, where they will eat fish, birds and other small creatures. They look very much like a crocodile at this point.

Cocoon

After four years, the wyrms come out of the water and form a cocoon. To look at, this cocoon is very much like a large log or even a small fallen tree. It is possible to walk past or even sit on the cocoon of a dragon without ever realising what it is.

The way to spot a dragon cocoon is by feeling the side that is touching the floor. There will be a very small pulse or movement coming from where the "log" meets the floor. It is during the cocoon stage that it is easiest to kill a dragon. Strangely, dragons in the cocoon stage are easily killed by fire. If you can make a fire around the cocoon you can cause the dragon to catch fire too. This will destroy the cocoon and the dragon inside, and save many human lives.

Dragon

Once a dragon has hatched from its cocoon it will have wings, be able to mate and be able to lay fresh eggs. This means the cycle will start all over again.

The Day the Dragon Came

I remember the day
The dragon came.

It filled the sky with
Burning fire
Landing on the hillside
Setting the whole world
Ablaze.

The trees, the fields, the farms
All burning!
The houses, the cottages, the barns
All burning!

Everyone went running,
But one man was standing –
Still.
His sword was in his hand,
His helmet on his head –
Standing!

The dragon came,
The roaring flame,
The flash of blade
The clash it made!
The dragon stopped
Its head was dropped
For blade had cleanly cut it!

Our hero true,
Had killed the beast,
But none could feast,
For all around the flames were
Spread
And so our homes were
Ended.

Niggle's Bad Day

"Stop that!" shouted the teacher. Niggle stopped what he was doing and looked around at his teacher, who was now stomping towards him. What had he done wrong? What was she going to say now?

Mrs Forg stopped just in front of Niggle and drew herself up. She stretched out her long neck, snapped her jaws and beat her wings. Niggle stepped backwards and tripped over his tail. The other dragons laughed out loud.

Flames sprang from Mrs Forg's snout and the class stopped laughing. Everyone turned back to their work. Niggle got to his feet and looked up at Mrs Forg.

"You are meant to be trying to set fire to your own knight," Mrs Forg said, looking down at the little dragon, "not trying to set fire to your best friend's work!"

"I wasn't… I was just…" Niggle felt hot all over. He had not been trying to set fire to Miggs' work. Miggs had called his name and he had looked around just as he was about to set fire to his own model knight. This was so unfair!

Mrs Forg was now glaring so fiercely at Niggle that he thought she might eat him. He had heard stories from his older brother about teachers who had eaten their pupils. He hadn't believed him then… but now he was not so sure.

"Just keep your flames on your own model knight," cried Mrs Forg as she turned and stomped away.

Miggs leaned over. "Yeah! Just keep your flames on your own model knight!" he whispered, grinning.

"Yeah, yeah! Very funny!" replied Niggle. He breathed in hard and then blew thick smoke out of his mouth at his model knight. He had spent the last week making the model in class. He was not sure he wanted to set it on fire.

Next to him, Miggs' knight was now blazing away. The straw inside his pieces of armour was properly alight and beginning to crackle.

Niggle took another breath and pushed out harder this time. Suddenly flames burst from his mouth and within moments his knight was on fire too.

Key Stage 1

Set B

English reading

Paper 2: reading answer booklet

First Name	
Last Name	

(page 79)

1 How can this guide help you if a dragon comes to your neighbourhood?

_____

1 mark

(page 79)

2 What is the first thing you should do if you see a dragon?

_____

1 mark

(page 79)

3 Write **two** things you should **not** do if you see a dragon.

1. _____

2. _____

1 mark

(page 79)

4 **Find** and **copy two** reasons why dragons kill other dragons.

1. _____

2. _____

(page 79)

5 *Their heads are similar to a crocodile's — they have a long snout filled with razor-sharp teeth.*

Find and **copy one** word that means *nose*.

_____

(page 80)

6 Draw **three** lines to match these dragons to what the text says about them.

Green dragons	•	•	eat sheep or cows
Black dragons	•	•	the cleverest of all dragons
Blue dragons	•	•	some have two heads

1 mark

1 mark

1 mark

7 Put ticks in the table to show which sentences are **true** and which are **false**.

Sentence	True	False
Only some dragons hatch from eggs.		
Wyrms come out of the water to form a cocoon.		
It is hardest to kill a dragon when it is in the cocoon stage.		
Dragons newly hatched from cocoons do not have wings.		

2 marks

(page 82)

8 What landed on the hillside?

Tick **one**.

a dragon ☐

a knight ☐

a man ☐

a tree ☐

1 mark

(page 82)

9 How do you know the man who fought the dragon was a knight?

_____

1 mark

(page 82)

10 Explain why the people could not feast and celebrate the death of the dragon.

_____

_____

_____

2 marks

(page 83)

11 How did Niggle trip over his tail?

Tick **one**

He swung round. ☐

He stepped backwards. ☐

He hid from the teacher. ☐

He sat on his chair. ☐

1 mark

(page 83)

12 What came out of Mrs Forg's snout to make the class stop laughing?

_____

1 mark

(pages 83–84)

13 What is the name of Niggle's best friend?

_____

1 mark

(page 83)

14 (a) The story shows that **Mrs Forg** was...

Tick **one**.

fun ☐   kind ☐

strict ☐   beautiful ☐

○ 1 mark

(page 84)

(b) The story shows that **Niggle** was...

Tick **one**.

naughty ☐   thoughtful ☐

angry ☐   unkind ☐

○ 1 mark

(page 84)

15 (a) How do you think Niggle felt at the end of the story?

_____

○ 1 mark

(page 84)

(b) Why did he feel like that?

_____

_____

○ 1 mark

(pages 83–84)

16   Number the following events from 1 to 5 to show the order that they

happened in the story.

The first one has been done for you.

      Niggle set fire to his model knight.   ☐

      Mrs Forg shouted, "Stop that!".   1

      Miggs set fire to his model knight.   ☐

      Niggle tripped over his tail.   ☐

      Niggle thought Mrs Forg might eat him.   ☐

1 mark

End of test

Key Stage 1

Set B

English grammar, punctuation and spelling

Paper 1: spelling

First Name	
Last Name	

Spelling

P.   We are at school _____.

---

1.   The _____ climbed the tree.   ◯

2.   The boat was _____ by pirates.   ◯

3.   The boy won the race because he was the _____.   ◯

4.   We went on holiday in the _____.   ◯

5.   I had to _____ a picture of a flower.   ◯

6.   The diamond was _____.   ◯

7.   They sang the _____ anthem for the Queen.   ◯

8.   I had a drink of orange _____.   ◯

9.   The _____ rolled down the hill.   ◯

10.   A _____ is smaller than a town.   ◯

11.   The _____ made a loud sound.   ◯

12.   I cooked a meal in the _____.   ◯

13.   I am _____ when eating chocolate.   ◯

14.   I _____ work hard at school.   ◯

15.   They walked _____ to school.   ◯

16.   The _____ burrowed in the mud.   ◯

17.   He was _____ for joy.   ◯

18.   _____ is a day of the week.   ◯

19.   London is the capital _____ of England.   ◯

20.   I had to _____ the present.   ◯

End of spelling test

BLANK PAGE

Key Stage 1

Set B

English grammar, punctuation and spelling

Paper 2: questions

First Name	
Last Name	

Practice questions

a Write one word on the line below to complete the sentence in the past tense.

The children _____ on the climbing frame yesterday.

b Circle the **noun** in the sentence below.

The steps were slippery.

1 Tick the **noun phrase** below.

Tick **one**.

the small dog ☐

so quietly ☐

will be playing ☐

very cold ☐

1 mark

2 Tick the correct word to complete the sentence below.

We can play outdoors _____ the weather is good.

Tick **one**.

but ☐

if ☐

or ☐

however ☐

1 mark

3 What type of sentence is below? The end punctuation is covered.

My favourite toy is my blue robot

Tick **one**.

a question ☐

a command ☐

an exclamation ☐

a statement ☐

1 mark

4 Add **two** letters to the word <u>helpful</u> to make a word that means <u>not</u> <u>helpful</u>.

I was very busy and Daniel was playing football. He was very _____helpful.

1 mark

5 Add a **suffix** to the word <u>small</u> to complete the sentence below.

I am the small_____ child in my class.

1 mark

6 Circle the **two** adverbs in the sentence below.

I gently rocked the baby as she screamed loudly.

1 mark

7 Freya and Oscar were finding out about dinosaurs.

Write a **question** they could ask their teacher in the speech bubble.

Remember to use correct punctuation.

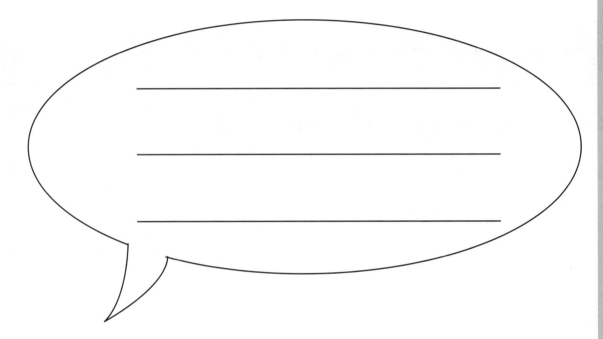

2 marks

8 What type of word is underlined in the sentence below?

The dog barked at the <u>mouse</u>.

Tick **one**.

a verb ☐

a noun ☐

an adjective ☐

an adverb ☐

1 mark

9 Which sentence is a **command**?

Tick **one**.

Will you be quiet please? ☐

That is too noisy! ☐

Be quiet now. ☐

You are being too noisy. ☐

1 mark

10 Add a **question mark** or an **exclamation mark** to complete each sentence below.

How many legs does a duck have ☐

What a fantastic painting ☐

Why are you crying ☐

1 mark

11 Circle the **verb** in the sentence below.

Ahmed ran to his wooden peg.

1 mark

12 Tick the sentence that shows what the child is doing now.

Tick **one**.

The child played on the swing. ☐

The child is playing on the swing. ☐

The child wanted to play on the swing. ☐

The child was playing on the swing. ☐

1 mark

13 Tick the **two** nouns in the sentence below.

I walked happily to school in the beautiful sunshine.

1 mark

14 Why do the underlined words start with a **capital letter**?

It was the first day of September. The sun was shining. The children were excited to start school.

_____

_____

1 mark

15 Add one **comma** to the sentence below in the correct place.

Rachel Freddie and Harley won the relay race.

1 mark

16 Look at where the arrow is pointing.

We cant go to the cinema today because it is closed.
↑

Which punctuation mark is needed?

Tick **one**.

a comma ☐

an apostrophe ☐

a full stop ☐

an exclamation mark ☐

1 mark

17 Write the words <u>could not</u> as one word, using an **apostrophe**.

I <u>could not</u> eat all of my lunch.

↓

[   ]

18 Write an **apostrophe** in the correct place in the sentence below.

T h a t   i s   T i m s   b i k e .

19 Which sentence is written in the **present tense**?

Tick **one**.

Sam went for a ride on his bike. ☐

Sam rides on his bike. ☐

Sam had a ride on his bike. ☐

Sam rode on his bike. ☐

1 mark

End of test

Notes

Notes

Notes

Acknowledgements

The author and publisher are grateful to the copyright holders for permission to use quoted materials and images.

All Images are © Shutterstock.com and © Collins Education

Every effort has been made to trace copyright holders and obtain their permission for the use of copyright material. The author and publisher will gladly receive information enabling them to rectify any error or omission in subsequent editions. All facts are correct at time of going to press.

Published by Collins
An imprint of HarperCollinsPublishers

1 London Bridge Street
London SE1 9GF

© HarperCollinsPublishers Limited 2018

ISBN 9780008318819

First published 2018

10 9 8 7 6 5 4 3 2 1

British Library Cataloguing in Publication Data.

A CIP record of this book is available from the British Library.

Author: Rachel Axten-Higgs
Commissioning Editor: Alison James
Editor and Project Manager: Katie Galloway
Cover Design: Paul Oates
Inside Concept Design: Ian Wrigley
Text Design and Layout: Aptara® Inc
Production: Lyndsey Rogers
Printed in the UK by Martins The Printers